THE SECRET

OF

INTERCESSION

ANDREW MURRAY

THE SECRET
OF
INTERCESSION

ANDREW MURRAY

CHRISTIAN · LITERATURE · CRUSADE
Fort Washington, Pennsylvania 19034

CHRISTIAN LITERATURE CRUSADE

U.S.A.
P.O. Box 1449, Fort Washington, PA 19034

GREAT BRITAIN
51 The Dean, Alresford, Hants., SO24 9BJ

AUSTRALIA
P.O. Box 419M, Manunda, QLD 4879

NEW ZEALAND
10 MacArthur Street, Feilding

ISBN 0-87508-825-2

Copyright © 1998
Christian Literature Crusade
U.S.A.

This new revised American edition 1998

This printing 2000

Cover Design: Skip Mable Studios
Cover photo credit: Peggy Hurd

PRINTED IN THE UNITED STATES OF AMERICA

INTRODUCTION

THIS little book has been prepared with the view of rousing Christians to some right sense of the solemn duty, of the high privilege, and of the wonderful power of intercession. It seeks to point out what place intercession has in God's plan for the extension of His kingdom, and for the strengthening of the life of His children so that they may receive from Him the heavenly blessings He has to bestow and then go forth to impart them to the world around.

The Dutch original has been found helpful in encouraging Christians to realize their high calling and in helping them to take their place among the Lord's remembrancers who call upon Him day and night. This translation is issued with the hope and prayer that it may be used in Bible Classes and Prayer Meetings to foster that spirit of devotion and prayer which is so essential to the Christian life.

ANDREW MURRAY

Intercession

"Pray one for another."—James 5:16.

WHAT a mystery of glory there is in prayer! On the one hand we see God, in His holiness and love and power, waiting, longing to bless man; and on the other, sinful man, a worm of the dust, bringing down from God by prayer the very life and love of heaven to dwell in his heart.

But how much greater the glory of intercession!—when a man makes bold to say to God what he desires for others, and seeks to bring down on one soul, or it may be on hundreds and thousands, the power of the eternal life with all its blessings.

Intercession! Would one not say that this is the very holiest exercise of our boldness as God's children, the highest privilege and enjoyment connected with our intercourse with God—the power of being used by God as instruments for His great work of making men His habitation and showing forth His glory?

Would one not think that the Church would count intercession one of the chief means of grace and seek above everything else to cultivate in God's children the power of an unceasing prayerfulness on behalf of the perishing world?

Would one not expect that believers, having to some extent been brought into this divine secret, would feel what strength there is in unity of spirit and what assurance there is that God will certainly avenge His own elect who cry day and night to Him? It is when Christians cease from looking for the solution in mere external union and are, rather, bound together to the throne of God by an unceasing devotion to Jesus Christ which produces an unceasing continuance in supplication for the power of God's Spirit, that the Church will put on her beautiful garments, will put on her strength, and will overcome the world.

OUR gracious Father, hear our prayer and teach Thy Church; teach each of us what is the glory, what is the blessing, what is the all-prevailing power of inter-cession. Give us, we pray Thee, the vision of what intercession means to Thee, as essential for carrying out Thy blessed purpose; what it means to ourselves as the exercise of our royal priesthood; and what it will mean to Thy Church, and to perishing men, in the bringing down of the Spirit in power—for Jesus' sake. Amen.

THE OPENING OF THE EYES

"And Elisha prayed and said: Lord, open his eyes, that he may see. . . . And Elisha said, Lord, open the eyes of these men, that they may see."—2 Kings 6:17, 20.

HOW wonderfully the prayer of Elisha for his servant was answered! The young man saw the mountain full of chariots of fire and horsemen about Elisha. The heavenly host had been sent by God to protect His servant.

A second time Elisha prayed. The Syrian army had been smitten with blindness, and so was led into Samaria. There Elisha prayed for the opening of their eyes, and lo, they found themselves hopeless prisoners in the hand of the enemy.

We wish to use these prayers in the spiritual sphere, first of all, to ask that our eyes may see the wonderful provision that God has made for His Church in the baptism with the Holy Spirit. All the powers of the heavenly world are at our disposal in the service of the heavenly kingdom. How little the children of God live in the faith of that heavenly vision—the power of the Holy Spirit, on them, with them, and in them, for their own spiritual life, and as their strength joyfully to witness for their Lord and His work!

But we shall find that we need that second prayer too, that God may open the eyes of those of His children who do not as yet see the power which the world and sin have upon His people. They are as yet unconscious of the feebleness that marks the Church, making it impotent to do the work of winning souls for Christ and building up believers for a life of holiness and fruitfulness. Let us pray especially that God may open all eyes to see what the great and fundamental need of the Church is, in intercession to bring down His blessing, that the power of the Spirit may be known unceasingly in its divine efficacy and blessing.

OUR Father, which art in heaven, Thou who art so unspeakably willing to give us the Holy Spirit in power, hear our humble prayer. Open our eyes, we pray Thee, that we may realize fully the low estate of Thy Church and people, and as fully what treasures of grace and power Thou art willing to bestow in answer to the fervent prayer of a united Church. Amen.

THIRD DAY

Man's Place in God's Plan

"The heaven, even the heavens, are the Lord's; but the earth hath He given to the children of men."—Psalm 115:16.

GOD created heaven as a dwelling for Himself—perfect, glorious, and most holy. The earth He gave to man as his dwelling—everything very good, but only as a beginning, with the need of being kept and cultivated. The work God had done *man was to continue and perfect.* Think of the iron and the coal hidden away in the earth, of the steam hidden away in the water. It was left to man to discover and to use all this, as we see in the network of railways that span the world and the steamers that cover the ocean. God had created all to be thus used. He made the discovery and the use dependent on the wisdom and diligence of *man.* What the earth is today, with its cities and habitations, with its cornfields and orchards, it owes to man. The work God had begun and prepared was by man to be carried out in fulfillment of God's purpose. And so nature teaches us the wonderful partnership to which God calls man for the carrying out of the work of creation to its destined end.

This law holds equally true in the kingdom of grace. In this great redemp-

10

tion God has revealed the power of the heavenly life and the spiritual blessings of which heaven is full. *But He has entrusted to His people the work of making these blessings known, and making men partakers of them.*

What diligence the children of this world show in seeking for the treasures that God has hid in the earth for their use! Shall not the children of God be equally faithful in seeking for the treasures hid in heaven, to bring them down in blessing on the world? It is by the unceasing intercession of God's people that His kingdom will come and His will be done on earth as it is in heaven.

EVER blessed Lord, how wonderful is the place Thou hast given man, in trusting him to continue the work Thou hast begun. We pray Thee, open our hearts for the great thought that, through the preaching of the gospel and the work of intercession, Thy people are to work out Thy purpose. Lord, open our eyes—for Jesus' sake. Amen.

FOURTH DAY

INTERCESSION IN THE
PLAN OF REDEMPTION

"O Thou who hearest prayer, unto Thee shall all flesh come."—Psalm 65:2.

WHEN God gave the world into the power of man, made in His own image, who should rule over it as a viceroy under Him, it was His plan that Adam should do nothing but *with* God and *through* God, and God Himself would do all His work in the world through *Adam*. Adam was in very deed to be the owner, master, and ruler of the earth. When sin entered the world, Adam's power was proved to be a terrible reality, for through him the earth, with the whole race of man, was brought under the curse of sin.

When God made the plan of redemption, His object was to restore man to the place from which he had fallen. God chose His servants of old, who, through the power of intercession, could ask what they would and it should be given them. When Christ became man it was so that as man, both on earth and in heaven, He might intercede for man. And before He left the world, He imparted this right of intercession to His disciples: in the sevenfold promise of the Farewell Discourse (John 15—17) He declared that whatsoever they should ask He would do for them.

God's intense longing to bless seems in some sense to be graciously limited by His dependence on the intercession that rises from the earth. He seeks to rouse the spirit of intercession that He may be able to bestow His blessing on mankind. God regards intercession as the highest expression of His people's readiness to receive and to yield themselves wholly to the working of His almighty power.

Christians need to realize this as their true nobility and their only power with God—the right to claim and expect that God will hear prayer. It is only as God's children begin to see what intercession means in regard to God's kingdom that they will realize how solemn their responsibility is.

Each individual believer will be led to see that God waits for him to take his part. He will feel in very truth that the highest, the most blessed, the mightiest of all human instrumentalities for the fulfillment of the petition "as in heaven, so on earth," is the intercession that rises day and night, pleading with God for the power of heaven to be sent down into the hearts of men. Oh that God might burn into our hearts this one thought: Intercession in its omnipotent power is according to His will and is most certainly effectual!

FIFTH DAY

God Seeks Intercessors

"He saw that there was no man, and wondered that there was no intercessor."—
Isaiah 59:16.

FROM of old God had among His people intercessors to whose voice He had listened and given deliverance. Here we read of a time of trouble when He sought for an intercessor, but in vain. And He wondered! Think of what that means—the amazement of God that there should be none who loved the people enough or who had sufficient faith in His power to deliver, to intercede on their behalf. If there had been an intercessor He would have given deliverance; without an intercessor His judgments came down (see Isaiah 64:7; Ezek. 22:30–31).

Of what infinite importance is the place the intercessor holds in the kingdom of God! Is it not indeed a matter of wonder that God should give men such power, and yet that there are so few who know what it is to take hold of His strength and pray down His blessing on the world?

Let us try to realize the position. When God had in His Son produced the new creation and Christ had taken His place on the throne, the work of the extension of His kingdom was given into the hands of men. He ever liveth to pray;

prayer is the highest exercise of His royal prerogative as Priest-King upon the throne. All that Christ was to do in heaven was to be in fellowship with His people on earth. In His divine condescension God has willed that the working of His Spirit shall follow the prayer of His people. He waits for their intercession because that is the evidence of their preparation of heart—revealing to what extent they are ready to yield to His Spirit's control.

God rules the world and His Church through the prayers of His people. "That God should have made the extension of His kingdom to such a large extent dependent on the faithfulness of His people in prayer is a stupendous mystery and yet an absolute certainty." God calls for intercessors: in His grace He has made His work dependent on them; He waits for them.

OUR Father, open our eyes to see that Thou dost invite Thy children to have a part in the extension of Thy kingdom by their faithfulness in prayer and intercession. Give us such an insight into the glory of this holy calling that with our whole heart we may yield ourselves to its blessed service. Amen.

SIXTH DAY

Christ as Intercessor

"He is able to save them to the uttermost that come unto God by Him, seeing He ever liveth to make intercession for them."—Heb. 7:25.

WHEN God had said in Isaiah that He wondered that there was no intercessor, there followed the words: "Therefore His arm brought salvation unto Him. The Redeemer shall come to Zion" (Isaiah 59:16, 20). God Himself would provide the true intercessor, in Christ His Son, of whom it had already been said: "He bore the sin of many, and made intercession for the transgressors" (Isaiah 53:12).

In His life on earth Christ began His work as Intercessor. Think of the highpriestly prayer on behalf of His disciples and of all who should through them believe in His name. Think of His words to Peter, "I have prayed for thee, that thy faith fail not"—a proof of how intensely personal His intercession is. And on the cross He spoke as intercessor: "Father, forgive them."

Now that He is seated at God's right hand He continues, as our great High Priest, the work of intercession without ceasing. But with this difference: *that He gives His people power to take part in it.* Seven times in His Farewell Discourse He repeated the assurance that what they asked He would do.

The power of heaven was to be at their disposal. The grace and power of God waited for man's bidding. Through the leading of the Holy Spirit they would know what the will of God was. They would learn in faith to pray in His name. He would present their petition to the Father, and through His and their united intercession the Church would be clothed with the power of the Spirit.

BLESSED Redeemer, what wonderful grace that Thou callest us to share in Thy intercession! We pray Thee, arouse in Thy redeemed people a consciousness of the glory of this their calling, and of all the rich blessing which Thy Church in its impotence can, through its intercession in Thy name, bring down upon this earth. May Thy Holy Spirit work in Thy people a deep conviction of the sin of restraining prayer, of the sloth and unbelief and selfishness that is the cause of it, and of Thy loving desire to pour out the Spirit of prayer in answer to their petitions—for Thy name's sake. Amen.

SEVENTH DAY

THE INTERCESSORS GOD SEEKS

"I have set watchmen upon thy walls, O Jerusalem; they shall never hold their peace day nor night: ye that are the Lord's remembrancers, take ye no rest and give Him no rest."—Isaiah 62:6–7.

WATCHMEN are ordinarily placed on the walls of a city to give notice to the rulers of coming danger. God appoints watchmen not only to warn men—often they will not hear—but also to summon Him to come to their aid whenever a need or enemy may be threatening. The great mark of intercessors is to be that they are not to hold their peace day or night, to take no rest and to give God no rest, until the deliverance comes. In faith they may count upon the assurance that God will answer their prayer.

It is of this that our Lord Jesus said: "Shall not God avenge His own elect, who cry to Him day and night?" From every land the voice is heard that the Church of Christ, under the influence of the power of the world and the earthly-mindedness it brings, is losing its influence over its members. How feeble has become the evidence of God's presence in the conversion of sinners and the holiness of His people. With the great majority of Christians there is an utter neglect of Christ's call to take a part in the extension of His kingdom. The power of the Holy Spirit is but little experienced.

Amid all the discussions as to what can be done to interest young and old in the study of God's Word, or to awaken love for the services of His house, one hears but little of the indispensable necessity of the power of the Holy Spirit in the ministry and the membership of the Church. One sees but little sign of the conviction and confession that it is owing to the lack of prayer that the workings of the Spirit are so feeble; that only by united fervent prayer can a change be brought about. If ever there was a time when God's elect should cry day and night to Him, it is now. Will not you, dear reader, offer yourself to God for this blessed work of intercession? Will not you learn to count it the highest privilege of your life to be a channel through whose prayers God's blessing can be brought down to earth?

EVER blessed Father, hear us, we pray Thee, and do Thou Thyself raise up intercessors, such as Thou wouldst have. Give us, we beseech Thee, men and women to act as Thy remembrancers, taking no rest and giving Thee no rest, until Thy Church again be a praise in the earth. Blessed Father, let Thy Spirit teach us how to pray. Amen.

19

EIGHTH DAY

THE SCHOOL OF INTERCESSION

"Who in the days of His flesh, when He had offered up prayers and supplications with strong crying and tears, . . . and was heard in that He feared."—Heb. 5:7.

CHRIST, as Head, is Intercessor in heaven; we, as the members of His Body, are partners with Him on earth. Let no one imagine that it cost Christ nothing to become an intercessor. He could not without this be our example. What do we read of Him? (Isaiah 53:10–12):"When Thou shalt make *His soul an offering for sin,* He shall see His seed. . . . He shall see of *the travail of His soul.* . . . I will divide Him a portion with the great, because *He hath poured out His soul unto death."* Notice the thrice-repeated expression in regard to the pouring out of His soul.

The pouring out of the soul—that is the divine meaning of intercession. Nothing less than this was needed if His sacrifice and prayer were to have power with God. This giving of Himself over to live and die that He might save the perishing was a revelation as to the spirit that has power to prevail with God.

If we as helpers and fellow-laborers with the Lord Jesus are to share His power of intercession, there will need to be with us too the *travail of soul that there was with Him, the giving up of our life and its pleasures for the one supreme work of interceding for our fellow-men.* Intercession must not be a passing interest; it must become an ever-growing object of intense desire, for which above everything we long and live. It is the life of consecration and self-sacrifice that will indeed give power for intercession (Acts 15:26; 20:24; Phil. 2:17; Rev.12: 11).

The longer we study this blessed truth and think of what it means to exercise this power for the glory of God and the salvation of men, the deeper will become our conviction that it is worth giving up everything to take part with Christ in His work of intercession.

BLESSED Lord Jesus, be pleased to teach us how to unite with Thee in calling upon God for the souls Thou hast bought. Let Thy love fill us and all Thy saints, that we may learn to plead for the power of Thy Holy Spirit to be made known. Amen.

The Name of Jesus the Power of Intercession

"Hitherto have ye asked nothing in My name. In that day ye shall ask in My name; ask and ye shall receive, that your joy may be full."—John 16:24, 26.

DURING Christ's life upon earth the disciples had known but little of the power of prayer. In Gethsemane, Peter and the others had utterly failed. They had no conception of what it was to ask in the name of Jesus and to receive. The Lord promises them that in that day which was coming they would be able to pray with such a power in His name that they might ask what they would and it should be given to them.

"Hitherto nothing." *"In that day"* ye shall ask in *My* name and shall *receive."* These two conditions are still found in the Church. With the great majority of Christians there is such a lack of knowledge of their oneness with Christ Jesus, and of the Holy Spirit as the Spirit of prayer, that they do not even attempt to claim the wonderful promises Christ here gives. But where God's children know what it is to abide in vital union with Christ, and to yield to the Holy Spirit's teaching, they begin to learn that their intercession avails much and

that God will give the power of His Spirit in answer to their prayer.

It is faith in the power of Jesus' name, and our right to use it, that will give us the courage to follow on where God invites us to the holy office of intercessor. When our Lord Jesus, in His Farewell Discourse, gave His unlimited prayer promise, He sent the disciples out into the world with this consciousness: "He who sits upon the throne, and who lives in my heart, has promised that what I ask in His name I shall receive. *He will do it.*"

Oh, if Christians but knew what it is to yield themselves wholly and absolutely to Jesus Christ and His service, how their eyes would be opened to see that intense and unceasing prayerfulness is the essential mark of the healthy spiritual life; and that the power of all prevailing intercession will indeed be the portion of those who live only in and for their Lord!

BLESSED Saviour, give us the grace of the Holy Spirit so to live in Thee, and with Thee, and for Thee, that we may boldly look to Thee for the assurance that our prayers are heard. Amen.

TENTH DAY

Prayer the Work of the Spirit

"God has sent forth the Spirit of His Son into your hearts, crying, 'Abba, Father.' "— Gal. 4:6.

WE know what "Abba, Father" meant in the mouth of Christ in Gethsemane. It was the entire surrender of Himself to the very death, that the holy will of God's love in redemption of sinners might be accomplished. In His prayer He was ready for any sacrifice, even to the yielding of His life. In that prayer we have revealed to us the heart of Him whose place is at the right hand of God, the wonderful power of intercession that He exercises there, and His power to pour down the Holy Spirit.

It is to breathe the very spirit of His Son into our hearts that the Holy Spirit has been bestowed by the Father. Our Lord would have us yield ourselves as wholly to God as He did; to pray like Him, that God's will of love should be done on earth at any cost. As God's love is revealed in His desire for the salvation of souls, so also the desire of Jesus was made plain when He gave Himself for them. And He now asks of His people that that same love should fill them too, so that they give themselves wholly to the work of intercession and, at any cost, pray down God's love upon the perishing.

And lest anyone should think that this is too high and beyond our reach, *the Holy Spirit is actually given into our hearts* so that we may pray as Jesus did, in His power and in His name. It is the man who yields himself wholly to the leading of the Holy Spirit who will feel urged, by the compulsion of a divine love, to the undivided surrender to a life of continual intercession, because he knows that it is God who is working in him.

Now we can understand how Christ could give such unlimited promises of answer to prayer to His disciples: they were first going to be filled with the Holy Spirit. Now we understand how God can give such a high place to intercession in the fulfillment of His purpose of redemption: it is the Holy Spirit who breathes God's own desire into us *and enables us* to intercede for souls.

ABBA, Father! O grant that by Thy Holy Spirit there may be maintained in us the unceasing intercession for love for the souls for whom Christ died. Give, O give to Thy children the vision of the blessedness and the power which come to those who yield themselves to this high calling. Amen.

ELEVENTH DAY

CHRIST OUR EXAMPLE
IN INTERCESSION

"He shall divide the spoil with the strong, because . . . He bare the sin of many and made intercession for the transgressors."— Isaiah 53:12.

"HE made intercession for the transgressors." What did that mean to Him? Think of what it cost Him to pray that prayer effectually. He had to pour out His soul as an offering for sin and to cry in Gethsemane: "Father, Thy holy will of love be done."

Think what moved Him thus to sacrifice Himself to the very uttermost! It was His love to the Father—that His holiness might be manifest; and His love to souls—that they might be partakers of His holiness.

Think of the reward He won! As Conqueror of every enemy He is seated at the right hand of God, with the power of unlimited and assured intercession. And He would see His seed, a generation of those of the same mind with Himself, whom He could train to a share in His great work of intercession.

And what does this mean for us, when we indeed seek to pray for the transgressors? That we too yield ourselves wholly to the glory of the holiness and the love of the Father; that we too say, Thy will be done, cost what it may; that we too sacrifice ourselves, even to pouring out our soul unto death.

The Lord Jesus has in very deed taken us up into a partnership with Himself, in carrying out the great work of intercession. He in heaven and we on earth must have one mind, one aim in life— that we should, from love to the Father and to the lost, consecrate our lives to intercession for God's blessing. The burning desire of Father and Son for the salvation of souls must be the burning desire of our heart too.

What an honor! What a blessedness! And what a power for us to do the work because He lives and by His Spirit pours forth His love into our hearts!

EVERLASTING God of love, open our eyes to the vision of the glory of Thy Son, as He ever liveth to pray. And open our eyes to the glory of that grace which enables us in His likeness also to live that we may pray for the transgressors. Father, for Jesus' sake. Amen.

TWELFTH DAY

GOD'S WILL AND OURS

"Thy will be done."—Matt. 26:42.

IT is the high prerogative of God that everything in heaven and earth is to be done according to His will and as the fulfillment of His desires. When He made man in His image it was, above all, that his desires were to be in perfect accord with the desires of God. This is the high honor of being in the likeness of God—that we are to feel and wish just as God. In human flesh man was to be the embodiment and fulfillment of God's desires.

When God created man with the power of willing and choosing what he should be, He limited Himself in the exercise of His will. And when man had fallen and yielded himself to the will of God's enemy, God in His infinite love set about the great work of winning man back to making the desires of God his own. As in God, so in man, desire is the great moving power. And just as man had yielded himself to a life of desire after the things of the earth and the flesh, God had to redeem him and to educate him into a life of harmony with Himself. His one aim was that man's desire should be in perfect accord with His own.

The great step in this direction was

when the Son of the Father came into this world to reproduce the divine desires in His own human nature, and in His life and through prayer yield Himself up continually to the perfect fulfillment of all that God wished and willed. The Son, as man, said in agony and blood, "Thy will be done," and made the surrender even to being forsaken by God, that the power that had deceived man might be conquered and deliverance procured. It was in the wonderful and complete harmony between the Father and the Son when the Son said, "Thy will of love be done," that the great redemption was accomplished.

And now the great work of appropriating that redemption is this: that believers have to say first of all for themselves and then in lives devoted to intercession for others, "Thy will be done in heaven as on earth." As we plead for the Church—its ministers and its missionaries, its strong Christians or its young converts—and for the unsaved, whether nominally Christian or heathen, we have the privilege of knowing that we are *pleading for what God wills* and that through our prayers His will is to be done on earth as in heaven.

The Blessedness of a Life of Intercession

"Ye that are the Lord's remembrancers, take ye no rest and give Him no rest, till He make Jerusalem a praise in the earth."— Isaiah 62:6–7.

WHAT an unspeakable grace it is to be allowed to deal with God in intercession for the supply of the need of others!

What a blessing, in close union with Christ, to take part in His great work as Intercessor and to mingle my prayers with His! What an honor to have power with God in heaven over souls and to obtain for them what they do not know or think!

What a privilege, as a steward of the grace of God, to bring to Him the state of the Church or of individual souls, of the nearby ministers of the Word or His messengers far away in heathendom, and plead on their behalf till He entrusts me with the answer!

What blessedness, in union with other children of God, to strive together in prayer until the victory is gained over difficulties here on earth or over the powers of darkness in high places!

It is indeed worth living for, to know that God will use me as an intercessor to receive and dispense here on earth

His heavenly blessing and, above all, the power of His Holy Spirit.

This is in very deed the life of heaven: the life of the Lord Jesus Himself, in His self-denying love, taking possession of me and urging me to yield myself wholly to bear the burden of souls before Him and to plead that they may live.

Too long have we thought of prayer simply as a means for the supplying of our own needs in life and service. May God help us to see what a place intercession takes in His divine *counsel* and in His work for the *kingdom*. And may our hearts indeed feel that there is no honor or blessedness on earth at all equal to the unspeakable privilege of waiting upon God—bringing down from heaven and opening the way on earth for the blessing He delights to give!

O my Father, let Thy life indeed flow down to this earth and fill the hearts of Thy children! As the Lord Jesus pours out His love in His unceasing intercession in heaven, let it even be thus with us also upon earth—a life of overflowing love and never-ending intercession. Amen.

FOURTEENTH DAY

THE PLACE OF PRAYER

"These all continued with one accord in prayer and supplication."—Acts 1:14.

THE last words which Christ spoke before He left the world give us the four great notes of His Church: "Wait for the promise of the Father." "Ye shall receive power after that the Holy Spirit is come upon you." "Ye shall be witnesses unto Me." "Both in Jerusalem and unto the uttermost part of the earth."

United and unceasing prayer, the power of the Holy Spirit, living witnesses to the living Christ, from Jerusalem to the uttermost part of the earth—such are the marks of the true gospel, of the true ministry, of the true Church of the New Testament.

A Church of united and unceasing prayerfulness, a ministry filled with the Holy Spirit, the members being living witnesses to a living Christ, with a message to every creature on earth—such was the Church that Christ founded and such the Church that went out to conquer the world.

When Christ had ascended to heaven, the disciples knew at once what their work was to be: continuing with one accord in prayer and supplication. They were to be bound together, by the love and Spirit of Christ, into one Body. It

was this that gave them their wonderful power in heaven with God and upon
earth with men.

Their one duty was to wait in united
and unceasing prayer for the power of
the Holy Spirit, as the enduement from
on high for their witness to Christ to
the ends of the earth. A *praying* Church,
a *Spirit-filled* Church, a *witnessing*
Church, with *all the world* as its sphere
and aim—such is the Church of Jesus
Christ.

As long as it maintained this charac-
ter it had power to conquer. But alas,
as it came under the influence of the
world, how much it lost of its heavenly,
supernatural beauty and strength! How
unfaithful in prayer, how feeble the
workings of the Spirit, how formal its
witness to Christ, and how unfaithful
to its worldwide mission!

*BLESSED Lord Jesus, have mercy upon
Thy Church, and give, we pray Thee, the
Spirit of prayer and supplication as of
old, that Thy Church may prove what
power from Thee rests upon her and her
testimony for Thee, to win the world to
Thy feet. Amen.*

Paul as an Intercessor

"I bow my knees unto the Father, that He would grant you to be strengthened with might by His Spirit."—Eph. 3:14, 16.

WE think of Paul as the great missionary, the great preacher, the great writer, the great Apostle "in labors more abundant." We do not sufficiently think of him as the intercessor who sought and obtained, by his supplication, the power that rested upon all his other activities and brought down the blessing that rested on the churches that he served.

We see above what he wrote to the Ephesians. Think of what he said to the Thessalonians (1 Thess. 3:10, 13): "Night and day praying exceedingly, that we might perfect that which is lacking in your faith, to the end He may establish your hearts unblameable in holiness." To the Romans (chap. 1:9): "Without ceasing I make mention of you always in my prayers." To the Philippians (chap. 1:4): "Always in every prayer of mine for you all, making request with joy." And to the Colossians (chap. 1:9; 2:1) "We do not cease to pray for you. I would that ye knew what great conflict I have for you."

Day and night he cried to God in his intercession for them, that the light and the power of the Holy Spirit might be in

34

them; and as earnestly as he believed in the power of his intercession for them, so also did he believe in the blessing that theirs would bring upon him. "I beseech you, that ye strive together with me in your prayers to God for me" (Rom. 15:30). "God will yet deliver us, ye also helping together by prayer for us" (2 Cor. 1:10–11). "Praying also for me, that I may open my mouth boldly" (Eph. 6:18–19; Col. 4:3; 2 Thess. 3:1). "This shall turn to my salvation through your prayer" (Phil. 1:19).

The whole relationship between pastor and people depends on united continual prayerfulness. Their whole relationship to each other is a heavenly one, spiritual and divine, and can only be maintained by unceasing prayer. It is when ministers and people waken up to the consciousness that the power and blessing of the Holy Spirit is waiting for their united and unceasing prayer, that the Church will begin to know something of what apostolic Christianity is.

EVER-BLESSED Father, we do most humbly beseech Thee, restore again graciously to Thy Church the spirit of supplication and intercession—for Jesus' sake. Amen.

SIXTEENTH DAY

Intercession for Laborers

"The harvest truly is plenteous, but the laborers are few; pray ye therefore the Lord of the harvest, that He will send forth laborers into His harvest."—Matt. 9:37–38.

THE disciples understood very little of what these words meant. Christ gave them as a seed-thought, to be lodged in their hearts for later use. At Pentecost, as they saw how many of the new converts were ready in the power of the Spirit to testify of Christ, they must have felt how the ten days of continuous united prayer had brought this blessing too, as the fruit of the Spirit's power—laborers in the harvest.

Christ meant to teach us that however large the field may be, and however few the laborers, prayer is the best, the sure, the only means for supplying the need.

What we need to understand is that it is not only in time of need that the prayer must be sent up, but that the whole work is to be carried on in the spirit of prayer, so that the prayer for laborers will be in perfect harmony with the whole of our life and effort.

In the China Inland Mission, when the number of missionaries had gone up to 200, at a conference held in China they felt so deeply the need of more laborers for districts quite unprovided for that, after much prayer, they felt at liberty to ask God to give them within a year 100 additional laborers and £10,000 to meet the expenses. They agreed to continue in prayer day by day throughout the year. At the end of the time the 100 suitable men and women had been found, with £11,000.

To meet the need of the world, its open fields and its waiting souls, the churches all complain about the lack of laborers and of funds. Does not Christ's voice call us to the united and unceasing prayer of the first disciples? God is faithful, by the power of His Spirit, to supply every need. Let the Church take the posture of united prayer and supplication. God hears prayer.

BLESSED Lord Jesus, teach Thy Church what it means so to live and labor for Thee, in the Spirit of unceasing prayer-fulness, that our faith may rise to the assurance that Thou wilt in very deed, in a way surpassing all expectation, meet the crying need of a dying world. Amen.

SEVENTEENTH DAY

INTERCESSION FOR INDIVIDUAL SOULS

"Ye shall be gathered one by one, O ye children of Israel."—Isaiah 27:12.

IN our body, every member has its appointed place. So it is, too, in society and in the Church. The work must always aim at the welfare and the highest perfection of the whole, through the cooperation of every individual member.

In the Church the thought is found too often that the salvation of men is the work of the minister. However, he generally deals only with the crowd and seldom reaches the individual. This is the cause of a twofold evil. The individual believer does not understand that it is necessary for him to testify to those around him—not only for the ingathering of souls but for the nourishment and the strengthening of his own spiritual life as well. And unconverted souls suffer unspeakable loss because Christ is not personally brought to them by each believer they meet.

The thought of intercession for those around us is all too seldom found. Its restoration to its right place in the Christian life—how much that would mean to the Church and its missions! Oh, when will Christians learn the great truth that "what God in heaven desires to do *needs prayer on earth as its indispensable condition.*" As we realize this, we shall discover that intercession is the chief element in the conversion of souls. All our efforts are vain without the power of the Holy Spirit given in answer to prayer. It is when ministers and people unite in a covenant of prayer and testimony that the Church will flourish. Oh that every believer might understand the part he has to take!

And what can we do to stir up the spirit of intercession? There is a twofold answer. Let every Christian, as he begins to get an insight into the need and the power of intercession, make a start in the exercise of it on behalf of single individuals. Pray for your children, for your relatives and friends, for all with whom God brings you into contact. If you feel that you lack the power to intercede, let this discovery humble you and drive you to the mercy seat. *God wants every redeemed child of His to intercede for the perishing.* It is the vital breath of the normal Christian life and the proof that one is born from above.

So pray intensely and persistently that God may bestow the power of His Holy Spirit on you and to His children around you. Then the power of intercession will have the place that God can honor.

EIGHTEENTH DAY

INTERCESSION FOR MINISTERS

"And for me."—Eph. 6:19. *"Praying also for us."*—Col. 4:3. *"Finally, brethren, pray for us."*—2 Thess. 3:1.

THESE expressions of Paul's suggest what the strength of his conviction must have been—that the Christians had power with God, and that their prayer would in very deed bring new strength to him in his work. Because of his sense of the actual unity of the Body of Christ and of the interdependence of each member, humble or honorable, on the life that flowed through the whole Body, he seeks to rouse Christians, both for their sakes and his, and especially for the sake of the kingdom of God, with his call: "Continue in prayer, and watch in the same with thanksgiving, meanwhile praying also for us."

The Church depends upon the ministry to an extent that we very little realize. The place of the minister is so high—a steward of the mysteries of God and an ambassador for God who beseeches men in Christ's name to be reconciled to Him—that unfaithfulness or inefficiency must bring a terrible blight on the Church that he serves. If Paul, after having preached for twenty years in the power of God, still needed the prayer of the Church, how much more does the ministry in our day need it?

The minister needs the prayer of his people. He has a right to it. He is in very truth dependent on it. *It is his task to train Christians for their work of intercession on behalf of the Church and the world.* He must begin by training them to pray for *him.* And he may need to begin still farther back and learn personally to pray more for himself and for them.

Let all intercessors who are seeking to enter more deeply into their blessed work give a larger place to the ministry, both of their own church and of other churches. Let them plead with God for individual men and for special circles. Let them continue in prayer and watch therein, that ministers may be men of power, men of prayer, and full of the Holy Spirit. O brethren, pray for the ministry!

OUR Father which art in heaven, we humbly pray Thee to arouse believers to a sense of their calling to pray for the ministers of the gospel in the spirit of faith. Amen.

NINETEENTH DAY

PRAYER FOR ALL SAINTS

"With all prayer and supplication praying at all seasons in the Spirit, and watching thereunto in all perseverance and supplication for all the saints."—Eph. 6:18.

NOTICE how Paul repeats the words in the intensity of his desire to reach the hearts of his readers. "With all prayer and supplication praying at all seasons, watching thereunto in all perseverance and all supplication." It is "*all* prayer, *all* seasons, *all* perseverance, *all* supplication." The words claim thought if they are to meet with the needed response.

Paul felt so deeply the unity of the Body of Christ, and was so sure that this unity could be realized only in the exercise of love and prayer, that he pleaded with the believers at Ephesus unceasingly and fervently to pray for all saints—not only those in their immediate circle but any of whom they might hear. "Unity is strength." As we today exercise this power of intercession with all perseverance, we shall be delivered from self with all its feeble prayers and lifted up to an enlargement of heart in which the love of Christ can flow freely and fully through us.

The great lack in true believers often is that in prayer they are occupied with themselves and with what God must do for them. Let us realize that we have here a call to every believer to give himself without ceasing to the exercise of love and prayer. It is as we forget ourselves, trusting that God will take charge of us, and yield ourselves to the great and blessed word of calling down the blessing of God on our brethren, that the whole Church will be fitted to do its work in making Christ known to every creature. This alone is the healthy and the blessed life of a child of God who has yielded himself wholly to Christ Jesus.

Pray for God's children and the Church around you. Pray for all the work in which they are engaged, or ought to be. Pray at all seasons in the Spirit for all God's saints. There is no blessedness greater than that of abiding communion with God. And there is no way that leads to the enjoyment of this more surely than the life of intercession for which these words of Paul appeal so pleadingly.

TWENTIETH DAY

MISSIONARY INTERCESSION

"When they had fasted and prayed, and laid their hands on them, they sent them away."—Acts 13:3.

"HOW to multiply the number of Christians who will individually and collectively wield this force of intercession for the conversion and transformation of men—*that is the supreme question of Foreign Missions.* Every other consideration and plan is secondary to that of wielding the forces of prayer.

"That those who love this work, and bear it upon their hearts, will follow the scriptural injunction to pray unceasingly for its triumph, we take for granted. To such, not only the morning watch and the hours of stated devotion, but all times and seasons will witness an attitude of intercession that refuses to let God go until He crown His workers with victory."

Missions have their root in the love of Christ, as that was proved on the cross and now lives in our heart. As men are so earnest in seeking to carry out God's plans for the natural world, so God's children should be at least as wholehearted in seeking to bring Christ's love to all mankind. Intercession is the chief means appointed by God to bring the great redemption within the reach of all.

Pray for the missionaries, that the Christ-life in them may be clear and strong; that they may be men of prayer and filled with love, in whom the power of the spiritual life is made manifest.

Pray for the native Christians, that they may know the glory of the mystery among the heathen: Christ in them, the hope of glory.

Pray for the baptism classes and all the pupils in schools, that the teaching of God's Word may be in power. Pray especially for the native pastors and evangelists, that the Holy Spirit may fill them to be witnesses for Christ among their fellow-countrymen.

Pray, above all, that the Church of Christ may be lifted out of its indifference and that every believer may be brought to understand that the one object of his life is to help to make Christ King on the earth.

OUR gracious God, our eyes are unto Thee. Wilt Thou not in mercy hear our prayer, and by the Holy Spirit reveal the presence and the power of Christ in the work of Thy servants? Amen.

TWENTY-FIRST DAY

THE GRACE OF INTERCESSION

"Continue in prayer, and watch in the same with thanksgiving, praying also for us."—Col. 4:2–3.

THERE is nothing that can bring us nearer to God and lead us deeper into His love than the work of intercession. There is nothing that can give us a higher experience of the likeness of God than the power of pouring out our hearts into the bosom of God in prayer for men around us. There is nothing that can so closely link us to Jesus Christ, the great Intercessor, and give us the experience of His power and Spirit resting on us, as the yielding of our lives to the work of bringing the great redemption into the hearts and lives of our fellow-men. There is nothing in which we shall know more of the powerful working of the Holy Spirit than the prayer breathed by Him into our hearts, "Abba, Father," in all the fullness of meaning that it had for Christ in Gethsemane. There is nothing that can so help us to prove the power and the faithfulness of God to His Word as when we reach out in intercession to the multitudes, either in the Church of Christ or in the darkness of heathenism. As we pour out our souls as a living sacrifice before God, with the one persistent plea that He shall, in answer to our prayer, open the windows of heaven and send down His abundant blessing, God will be glorified, our souls will reach their highest destiny, and God's kingdom will come.

There is nothing that will so help us to understand and to experience the living unity of the Body of Christ, and the irresistible power that it can exert, as the daily and continued fellowship with God's children in the persistent plea that God will arise and have mercy upon Zion and make her a light and a life to those who are sitting in darkness. O my brother, O my sister, how little we realize what we are *losing* in not living in fervent intercession! What may we not *gain* for ourselves and for the world if we allow God's Spirit, as a Spirit of grace and of supplication, to master our whole being!

In heaven Christ lives to pray; His whole intercourse with His Father is prayer—an asking and receiving of the fullness of the Spirit for His people. God delights in nothing so much as in prayer. Shall we not learn to believe that the highest blessings of heaven will be unfolded to us as we pray more?

BLESSED Father, pour down the Spirit of supplication and intercession on Thy people—for Jesus Christ's sake. Amen.

TWENTY-SECOND DAY

UNITED INTERCESSION

"There is one Body, and one Spirit."—Eph. 4:4.

OUR own bodies teach us how essential for their health and strength it is that every member should take its full share in seeking the welfare of the whole. It is even so in the Body of Christ. There are, alas, too many who look upon salvation only in connection with their own happiness. There are those, again, who know that they live not unto themselves and truly seek in prayer and work to bring others to share in their happiness; but even many of them do not yet understand that in addition to their personal circle or church, they have a calling to enlarge their hearts to take the whole Body of Christ Jesus into their love and their intercession.

Yet this is what the Spirit and the love of Christ will enable them to do. It is only when intercession *for the whole Church, by the whole Church*, ascends to God's throne, that the Spirit of unity and of power can have its full sway. The desire that has been awakened for closer union between the different branches of the Church of Christ is cause for thanksgiving. And yet the difficulties are so great and, in the case of different nationalities of the world, so apparently insuperable, that the thought of a united Church on earth appears beyond reach.

Let us bless God that there is a unity in Christ Jesus deeper and stronger than any visible manifestation could make it; and that there is a way in which even now, midst all diversity of administrations, this unity can be practically exemplified and utilized as the means of an unthought-of accession of divine strength and blessing in the work of the kingdom. *It is in the cultivation and increase of the Spirit and in the exercise of intercession that this true unity can be realized.* As believers are taught what is the meaning of their calling as a royal priesthood, they will be led to see that God is not confined in His love or promises to their limited spheres of labor. He invites them to enlarge their hearts and, like Christ and the apostle Paul, to pray for all who believe, or can yet be brought to believe, that this earth and the Church of Christ in it will by intercession be bound to the throne of heaven as it has never yet been.

Let Christians and ministers agree and bind themselves together for this worldwide intercession. It will strengthen the confidence that prayer will be heard, and that their prayers, too, will become indispensable for the coming of the kingdom.

TWENTY-THIRD DAY

UNCEASING INTERCESSION

"Pray without ceasing."—1 Thess. 5:17.

HOW different is the standard of the average Christian, with regard to a life in the service of God, from that which Scripture gives us. In the former the chief thought is personal safety—grace to pardon our sin and to live such a life as may secure our entrance into heaven. How high above this is the Bible standard—a Christian surrendering himself with all his powers, with his time and thought and love wholly yielded to the glorious God who has redeemed him and whom he now delights in serving, in whose fellowship is heaven begun.

To the former the command "Pray without ceasing" is simply a needless and impossible life of perfection. Who can do it? We can get to heaven without it. To the true believer, on the contrary, it holds out the promise of the highest happiness, of a life crowned by all the blessings that can be brought down on souls around through his intercession. And as he perseveres, it becomes increasingly his highest aim upon earth, his highest joy, his highest experience of the wonderful fellowship with the holy God.

"Pray without ceasing!" Let us take that word in a large faith, as a promise of what God's Spirit will work in us—of how close and intimate our union to the Lord Jesus can be, and our likeness to Him, in His ever-blessed intercession at the right hand of God. Let it become to us one of the chief elements of our heavenly calling to be consciously the stewards and administrators of God's grace to the world around us. As we think of how Christ said, "I in them, and Thou in Me," let us believe that just as the Father worked in Him, *so Christ, the interceding High Priest, will work and pray in us*. As the faith of our high calling fills our hearts, we shall begin literally to feel that there is nothing on earth for one moment to be compared with the privilege of being God's priests, walking without intermission in His holy presence, bringing the burden of the souls around us to the footstool of His throne, and receiving at His hands the power and blessing to dispense to our fellow-men.

This is indeed the fulfillment of the word of old, "Man created in the likeness and the image of God."

TWENTY-FOURTH DAY

Intercession the Link between Heaven and Earth

"Thy will be done, as in heaven, so on earth."—Luke 11:2.

WHEN God created heaven and earth, He meant heaven to be the divine pattern to which earth was to be conformed. "As in heaven, so on earth" was to be the law of its existence.

This truth calls us to think of what constitutes the glory of heaven. God is all in all there: everything lives in Him and to His glory. But think of what this earth has become, with all its sin and misery: the vast majority of the race without any knowledge of the true God and the remainder nominal Christians. Most of the latter are utterly indifferent to His claims, estranged from His holiness and love. What a revolution, what a miracle is needed if the word is to be fulfilled: "As in heaven, so on earth."

And how is this ever to come true? *Through the prayers of God's children. Our Lord teaches us to pray for it! Intercession is to be the great link between heaven and earth.* The intercession of the Son, begun upon earth, continued in heaven, and carried on by His redeemed people upon earth, will bring about the mighty change: "As in heaven, so on earth." Christ said, "I come to do Thy will, O God," and ultimately prayed the great prayer in Gethsemane, "Thy will be done." Now His redeemed ones, who yield themselves fully to His mind and Spirit, can make His prayer their own and unceasingly send up the cry, "Thy will be done, as in heaven, so on earth."

Every prayer of a parent for a child, of a believer for the saving of the lost, or for more grace to those who have been saved, is part of the great unceasing cry going up day and night from this earth, "As in heaven, so on earth."

But it is when God's children not only learn to pray for their immediate circles and interests but enlarge their hearts to take in the whole Church and the whole world, that their united supplication will have power with God and hasten the day when it shall indeed be "as in heaven so on earth"—the whole earth filled with the glory of God. Child of God, will you not yield yourself, like Christ, to live with this one prayer: "Father, Thy will be done on earth as in heaven"?

OUR Father, which art in heaven, hallowed be Thy name, Thy kingdom come, Thy will be done—as in heaven, so on earth. Amen.

The Fulfillment of God's Desires

"The Lord hath desired Zion for His habitation. Here will I dwell; for I have desired it."—Psalm 132:13–14.

HERE you have the one great desire of God that moved Him in the work of redemption: His heart longed for man— to dwell with him and in him.

To Moses He said: "Let them make Me a sanctuary; that I may dwell among them." And just as Israel had to prepare the dwelling for God, even so His children are now called both to yield themselves for God to dwell in and to win others to become His habitation. As the desire of God towards us fills the heart, it will waken within us the desire to gather others around us to become His dwelling too.

What an honor! What a high calling, to count my worldly business as entirely secondary and to find my life and my delight in winning souls in whom God may find His heart's delight! "Here will I dwell; for I have desired it."

And this is what I can, above all, do through intercession: I can pray for God to give His Holy Spirit to those around me. It is God's great plan that man himself shall build Him a habitation. It is in answer to the unceasing intercession of His children that God will give His power and blessing. As this great desire of God fills us, we shall give ourselves wholly to labor for its fulfillment.

Think of David when he thought of God's desire to dwell in Israel. How he said: "I will not give sleep to my eyes, nor slumber to mine eyelids, until I find out a place for the Lord, an habitation for the mighty God of Jacob." And shall not we, to whom it has been revealed what that indwelling of God may be, give our lives for the fulfillment of His heart's desire?

Oh let us begin, as never before, to pray for our children, for the souls around us, and for all the world. And that not only because we love them but because God longs for them and gives us the honor of being the channels through whom His blessing is brought down. Children of God, awake to the realization of what it means that God is seeking to train you as intercessors, through whom the great desire of His loving heart can be satisfied!

O God, who hast said of human hearts, "Here will I dwell, for I have desired it," teach us, we pray Thee, to pray, day and night, that the desire of Thy heart may be fulfilled. Amen.

The Fulfillment of Man's Desire

"Delight thyself in the Lord, and He shall give thee the desires of thine heart."—Psalm 37:4.

GOD is love, an ever-flowing fountain, out of which streams the unceasing desire to make His creatures the partakers of all the holiness and the blessedness there is in Himself. This desire for the salvation of souls is in very deed God's perfect will, His highest glory.

This loving desire of God, to get His place in the heart of men, He imparts to all His children who are willing to yield themselves wholly to Him. It is in this that the likeness and image of God consist—to have a heart in which His love takes complete possession and leads us to find spontaneously our highest joy in loving as He does.

It is thus that our text finds its fulfillment: "Delight thyself in the Lord," and in His life of love, "and He will give thee the desires of thine heart." Count upon it that the intercession of love, rising up to heaven, will be met with the fulfillment of the desires of your heart. We may be sure that, as we delight in what God delights in, such prayer is inspired by God and will have its answer.

And our prayer becomes unceasingly, "Thy desires, O my Father, are mine. Thy holy will of love is my will, too."

In fellowship with Him we receive the courage, with our whole will and strength, to bring before His throne the persons or the circles in which we are interested, with an ever-growing confidence that our prayer will be heard. As we reach out in yearning love, we shall have the power to take hold of the will of God to bless, and to believe that God will work out His own blessed will in giving us the desires of our hearts—because the fulfillment of His desire has been the delight of our souls.

We then become, in the highest sense of the word, God's fellow-laborers. Our prayer becomes part of God's divine work of reaching and saving the lost. And we learn to find our happiness in losing ourselves in the salvation of those around us.

OUR Father, teach us that nothing less than delighting ourselves in Thee, and in Thy desires toward men, can inspire us to pray aright and give us the assurance of an answer. Amen.

My Great Desire

"One thing have I desired of the Lord, that will I seek after: that I may dwell in the house of the Lord all the days of my life, to behold the beauty of the Lord, and to inquire in His temple."—Psalm 27:4.

HERE we have man's response to God's desire to dwell in us. When the desire of God towards us begins to rule the life and heart, our desire is fixed on one thing, and that is, to dwell in the house of the Lord all the days of our life, to behold the beauty of the Lord, to worship Him in the beauty of holiness. Then we may inquire in His temple and learn what it means that God has said: "I the Lord have spoken it, and will do it. And I will yet for this be inquired of by the house of Israel to do it for them."

The more we realize the desire of God's love to give His rest in the heart and the more our desire is thus quickened to dwell every day in His temple and behold His beauty, the more the Spirit of intercession will grow upon us, to claim all that God has promised in His new covenant. Whether we think of our church and country, of our home and school, of our nearer or wider circle; whether we think of the saved and all their needs or the unsaved and their danger; whatever our concern, the thought that God is indeed longing to find His home and His rest in the hearts of men, if He be only "inquired of," will rouse our whole being to strive for Zion's sake not to hold our peace. All the thoughts of our feebleness and unworthiness will be swallowed up in the wonderful assurance that He has said of human hearts: "This is my rest for ever; here will I dwell, for I have desired it."

As our faith sees how high our calling is, how indispensable God has made fervent, intense, persistent prayer as the condition of His purpose being fulfilled, we shall be drawn to give up our life to a closer walk with God, to an unceasing waiting upon Him, and to a testimony to our brethren of what God will do in them and in us.

Is it not wonderful beyond all thought, this divine partnership in which God commits the fulfillment of His desires to our keeping? Shame upon us that we have so little realized it!

OUR Father in heaven, we beseech Thee, give, give in power, the Spirit of grace and supplication to Thy people—for Jesus' sake. Amen.

TWENTY-EIGHTH DAY

INTERCESSION DAY AND NIGHT

"Shall not God avenge His own elect, who cry day and night unto Him, though He bear long with them?"—Luke 18:7.

WHEN Nehemiah heard of the destruction of Jerusalem, he cried to God: "Hear the prayer of Thy servant which I pray before Thy face day and night." Of the watchmen set on the walls of Jerusalem, God said: "Who shall never hold their peace day nor night." And Paul writes (1 Thess. 3:10,13): "Night and day praying exceedingly, to the end He may establish your hearts unblameable in holiness before our God and Father."

Is such prayer night and day really needed and really possible? Most assuredly, when the heart is so supremely possessed by the desire that it cannot rest until this is fulfilled. The life has so come under the power of the heavenly blessing that nothing can keep it from sacrificing all to obtain it.

When a child of God begins to get a real vision of the need of the Church and of the world, a vision of the divine redemption which God has promised in the outpouring of His love into our hearts, a vision of the power of true intercession to bring down the heavenly blessing, a vision of the honor of being allowed as intercessors to take part in that work, it comes as a matter of course that he regards this work as the most heavenly upon earth—as an intercessor to cry day and night to God for the revelation of His mighty power.

Let us learn from David, who said: "The zeal of Thine house hath consumed me"; and from Christ our Lord, of whom these words were so intensely true. Let us learn that there is nothing so much worth living for as this one thought—how to satisfy the heart of God in His longing for human fellowship and affection, and how to win hearts to be His dwelling-place. And shall not we too give ourselves no rest until we have found a place for the Mighty One in our hearts and have yielded ourselves to the great work of intercession for so many after whom the desires of God are going out.

God grant that our hearts may be so brought under the influence of these divine truths that we may in very deed yield ourselves to make our devotion to Christ, and our longing to satisfy the heart of God, the chief object of our life.

LORD Jesus, the great Intercessor, who findest in this disposition all Thy glory, breathe, we pray Thee, of Thine own Spirit into our hearts—for Thy name's sake. Amen.

The High Priest and His Intercession

"We have such an High Priest, who is able to save them to the uttermost that come unto God by Him, seeing He ever liveth to make intercession for them."—Heb. 7:25–26; 8:1.

IN Israel, what a difference there was between the high priest and the priests and Levites. The high priest alone had access to the Holiest of All. He bore on his forehead the golden crown, engraved with "Holiness to the Lord," and by his intercession on the great Day of Atonement he bore the sins of the people. The priests brought the daily sacrifices, stood before the Lord, and came out to bless the people. The difference between high priest and priest was great. But still greater was the unity; they formed one body with the high priest, sharing with him the power to appear before God to receive and dispense His blessing to His people.

It is even so with our great High Priest. He alone has power with God, in a never-ceasing intercession, to obtain from the Father what His people need. And yet, infinite though the distance be between Him and the royal priesthood that surrounds Him for His service, the unity and the fellowship into which His

62

people have been taken up with Him is no less infinite than the apparent diversity. The blessing that He obtains from His Father for us, He holds for His people to receive from Him through their fervent supplication, to be dispensed to the souls among whom He has placed them as His witnesses and representatives.

As long as Christians simply think of being saved and of a life which will make that salvation secure, they never can understand the mystery of the power of intercession to which they are called.

But once they realize that salvation means a vital life-union with Jesus Christ—an actual sharing of His life dwelling and working in us and the consecration of our whole being to live and labor, to think and will, and to find our highest joy in living as a royal priesthood—the Church will put on her strength and prove, in intercourse with God and man, how truly the likeness and the power of Christ dwell in her.

OH that God would open our hearts to know and prove what our royal priesthood is: what the real meaning is of our living and praying in the name of Jesus, so that what we ask shall indeed be given us! O Lord Jesus, our Holy High Priest, breathe the spirit of Thine own holy priesthood into our hearts. Amen.

THIRTIETH DAY

A Royal Priesthood

"Call unto Me, and I will answer thee, and show thee great and mighty things which thou knowest not."—Jer. 33:3.

AS you plead for the great mercies of the new covenant to be bestowed, take with you these thoughts:

(1) The infinite willingness of God to bless. His very nature is a pledge of it. He delights in mercy. He waits to be gracious. His promises and the experience of His saints assure us of it.

(2) Why then does the blessing so often tarry? In creating man with a free will and making him a partner in the rule of the earth, God limited Himself. He made Himself dependent on what man would do. Man by his prayer would hold the measure of what God could do in blessing.

(3) Think of how God is hindered and disappointed when His children do not pray, or pray but little. The low, feeble life of the Church, the lack of the power of the Holy Spirit for conversion and holiness, is all owing to the lack of prayer. How different would be the state of the Church and of heathendom if God's people were to take no rest in calling upon Him!

(4) And yet God has blessed, just up to the measure of the faith and the zeal of His people. It is not for us to be content with this as a sign of His approval; rather, we

must say, If He has thus blessed our feeble efforts and prayers, what will He not do if we yield ourselves wholly to a life of intercession?

(5) Our lack of consecration has kept back God's blessing from the world. What a call this is to penitence and confession! He was ready to save men, but we were not willing for the sacrifice of a whole-hearted devotion to Christ and His service.

Children of God, God counts upon you to take your place before His throne as intercessors. Awake, I pray you, to the consciousness of your holy calling as a royal priesthood. Begin to live a new life in the assurance that intercession, in both the likeness to and the fellowship with the interceding Lord Jesus in heaven, is the highest privilege a man can desire. In this spirit take up the word with large expectations: "Call unto Me, and I will answer thee, and show thee great and mighty things which thou knowest not."

Let each one who has read thus far say whether he is not willing, whether he does not long to give himself wholly to this blessed calling, and in the power of Jesus Christ to make intercession—supplication for God's Church and people, and for a dying world—the one chief object of his life? Is this asking too much? Is it too much to yield your life for this holy service of the royal priesthood to that blessed Lord who gave Himself for us?

THIRTY-FIRST DAY

Intercession a Divine Reality

"And another angel came, . . . and there was given unto him much incense, that he should offer it with the prayers of all saints upon the golden altar which was before the throne."—Rev. 8:3.

ARE the thoughts to which this little book has given utterance not a sufficiently grave indictment of the subordinate place given to intercession in the teaching and practice of the Church, with its ministers and members? Is it not in very deed of such supreme importance as to make it an essential, altogether indispensable element in the true Christian life? To those who take God's Word in its full meaning, there can be no doubt about the answer.

Intercession is, by amazing grace, an essential element in God's redeeming purpose—so much so that without it the failure of its accomplishment may lie at our door. Christ's intercession in heaven is essential to His carrying out the work He began upon earth, but He also calls for the intercession of the saints in the attainment of His object. Just think of what we read: "All things are of God, who hath reconciled us to Himself by Jesus Christ, and hath given to us the ministry of reconciliation." As the reconciliation was dependent on Christ's doing His part, so in the accomplishment of the work He calls on the Church to do her part. We see how Paul regarded intercession day and night as indispensable to the fulfillment of the work that had been entrusted to him. It is but one aspect of that mighty power of God which works in the heart of His believing people.

Intercession is indeed a divine reality. Without it, the Church loses one of its chief beauties, loses the joy and the power of the Spirit-life for achieving great things for God. Without it, the command to preach the gospel to every creature can never be carried out. Without it, there is no power for the Church to recover from her sickly, feeble life and conquer the world. And in the life of the believer, minister or member, there can be no entrance into the abundant life and joy of daily fellowship with God except as he takes his place among God's select—the watchmen and remembrancers of God who cry to Him day and night.

Church of Christ, awake, awake! Listen to the call: "Pray without ceasing. Take no rest, and give God no rest." Let the answer be, even though it be with a sigh from the depths of the heart, "For Zion's sake will I not hold my peace." God's Spirit will reveal to us the power of a life of intercession as a divine reality, an essential and indispensable element of the great redemption, and therefore also of the true Christian life.

May God help us to know and to fulfill our calling!